About Michael Favala Goldman's writing:

Grounded and ethereal. Goldman's poems run the gamut: the pain, the pleasure, the awe, and the confusion of being. Deceptive meditations on everyday living reveal the greater truths of existence. A brilliant reminder of the magnitude experience.

– A.M. Larks, Kelp Journal

Goldman's poems leave us in a rich wake of stories, meanings, and contradictions inherent in being human. He transforms daily moments in fresh and playful ways, building poems everywhere, suggesting why a soul might stick around.

– Sharon Tracey, author of Land Marks

Michael Favala Goldman is a stealth poet. The plain language and deep meaning of his poems can reverberate to the core of your being.

– Lynette Yetter, Poetry Translation finalist 2023 PEN Awards

Goldman's poems are succinct and subtle, understated even, yet powerful and persuasive; one after another, they take the reader by quiet surprise.

– Barry DeCarli, author of Camouflage of Noise and Silence.

These are the poems we need in this human moment, at the sticky end of the pandemic. Goldman's transcendent vulnerability underscores how little we have, and how precious and resilient it is, after all.

– Sara Eddy, author of *Ordinary Fissures*

What sparkles in Goldman's work is that the voice is both sweet and edgy. There is a slight tone of annoyance, a touch of anger that compliments the quiet sweetness. The clash, the juxtaposition of these forces gives way to a voice that is proper. By 'proper' I mean *real,* a series of tropes that captures the nuances of the human experience, of the human tumble down the stairs of everyday life.

– Matthew Lippmann, author of *Mesmerizingly Sadly Beautiful,* winner of the Levis Prize in Poetry

We Are More Than Just This

Poems

Michael Favala Goldman

Cover illustrations by Susan Sensemann
ISBN: 978-81-19654-23-9

First Edition: 2024
Rs. 200/-

Cyberwit.net
HIG 45 Kaushambi Kunj, Kalindipuram
Allahabad - 211011 (U.P.) India
http://www.cyberwit.net
Tel: +(91) 9415091004
E-mail: info@cyberwit.net

Printed at Repro India Limited.

WITH APPRECIATION TO:

Jette, Linda and Libby, and to all the people, named and unnamed, who make appearances in this book. You help me to recognize the poetry in life.

Acknowledgments:

Vans *30 Poems In November, 2023*

That Day Arrived *Red Door Magazine, 2022-23*

The Gift; Luthier's Co-op: The Dream Window

Meat for Tea, summer, 2022

Perspective Function *Naugatuck River Review, 2023*

Fabrication *Wordpeace, 2023*

The spring I turned thirty-five and took up running

Sad Girls Club, 2023

At the Victory Bar and Grill

Red Ogre Review, Dec 2023

Fragment *Ariel Chart, Jan, 2024*

Author's Note

Poetry often creates discomfort – in the creator and in the observer – disturbance that pricks our ribcage, squeezes our heart, constricts our throat, echoes in our mind, plagues us with a kind of forced attention to what we otherwise would not notice, would rather not confront. We would prefer to get on with our day, with our benign distractions that keep us from seeing the cracks in our personalities, our unsatisfying connections, our subtle inconsistencies, our failings.

Some poetry reminds us we could use improvement; we have much to do. And that we ought to relish the chance. Often we do not, and then we may blame the poet for filling the world with dissonance, though the dissonance was there already. What the poetry has done is simply make us aware of it. Making the unconscious conscious is part of the poet's work. We may be bothered by poetry when it makes us realize – *I am this*. And then we realize: *We are more than just this.*

Michael Favala Goldman
Florence, MA
2024

Contents

1

At the Victory Bar and Grill

West Berlin, New Jersey

There is no sunken dining area
but there is a long table for twenty
set with coffee, decaf, and family, seated,
most wearing blue Happy Birthday tiaras
and purple Happy Birthday glitter hats.
A few have sunglasses, the party favor
since the poster says my stepfather
at eighty is still cool.

Among the group are several survivors
of cancer, heart disease, even a gunshot.
Everyone is recognizable, though many
have not seen each other in ten years.

The buffet makes no effort
to be more than edible, little round
pancakes, little round waffles,
thick, sticky fruit sauce, square scrapple
with creamed chipped beef, plain
bagels cut into pieces.

A lonely man makes omelets to order
for six or seven people waiting, standing
in a matrix according to some
predetermined formula.

The person with the cake arrives late
(she put the wrong information –Victory *Lane* –
into her GPS and ended up grousing
obscenities by a school in a nearby town)
and the diner staff scrounge up a baggie
with three birthday candles and a lighter.
The birthday boy looks jazzy in sunglasses
and purple glitter hat, and requests
a saxophone, of which there are none
to be had. The requisite song is sung.

Bottles of wine and gift cards are perused,
cake is sliced and eaten, leaving abstract
icing images of pink and brown on the
saucers. After fifty or so hugs goodbye,
probably also according to a predetermined
theory, guests seep out to the parking lot.
A few who like long goodbyes linger.
No one talks about next time.

Productive Constraint

You will not write a poem today.
You will travel by van-taxi with an old Carib
  who wants to do nothing on his birthday
  next Saturday, nothing at all! unless his
  only daughter invites him out for lunch
  which she has never done before in his life.
You will travel by open-air passenger ferry rocking
  through waves like an amusement park ride
  for the squeamish, on hard aluminum seats.
You will travel in the bed of a pick-up taxi
  on narrow switchback roads past goats,
  shorn sheep, a donkey in the ditch; no
  shoulders, beeps before blind corners.
You will stop suddenly at a postage stamp grocery
  to purchase your food for the next three meals
  in five minutes, not including seeded grapes
  $12.99 per bag or peanut butter at $11.99.
You will eat olive oil on packaged Cheesecake Factory
  brown bread for lunch, trail mix on the side.

Nyhavn

Copenhagen, Denmark
for writer Rolf Gjedsted (1947-2022)

I sit with you
on the concrete
edge of the canal,
while tourists
pass in boats,
walk by on the sidewalk,
and sit at cafe tables.

I am holding a bag
you have given me
with ten of your books.
I tell you I am traveling
with my wife, my son, and his fianceé.
You say, It must be nice
to have family.

In one hour,
part of your life
that could be passed on
is now mine, to pass on
to everyone else.

The spring I turned thirty-five and took up running

Cooper River Park, Cherry Hill, NJ
for my mother

I was standing with the river rats, everyone
saying what state of marriage or divorce
they were in, and I said I was divorced.

When it was his turn he said
I've never been married
and we all had a good chuckle.

I left a few notes on his windshield
with my phone number.
He never called.

I found out his last name; he was
two years older than me and living
at home with his parents.

So I called him there, spoke to his mother,
who thought it was a good idea
we go out on a date.

We saw *Annie Hall*, which I had seen
on a date with someone else the week before.
Next time he took me to a remote restaurant

in the Pine Barrens and ordered a plate
of frogs' legs. I overlooked that, and
asked him if he wanted to move in.

He didn't answer. Then one day
he pulled up in his orange Fiat
with all his belongings and never left.

This Afternoon

On the way to buy plumbing fixtures
for our bathroom remodel I was stuck
in construction traffic. My father called.

Coming through car speakers
gave him an air of omnipotence,
which he has too much of already.

In my field of vision was a row of huge
white trucks, cranes with workers up in
the power lines across the intersection.

My father went on at length about not wanting
to offend me, and of course I was entitled to
my own opinions, as my experience was not his.

But considering his extensive research, he wanted
to keep me safe. At this point I felt weird
electrical currents jagging through my body.

I said, into the windshield, I don't know
what you're referring to. Had he become
a burning bush along the state highway?

He said he was just concerned about my health,
that I shouldn't accept any more vaccines.
At that moment traffic started flowing again.

I told him, If you want to, you can find
validation for any opinion. I doubt that
meant to him what it meant to me.

Suddenly he was in a hurry to hang up.
I was in the parking lot. My legs were shaky.
I needed a faucet, glass shelves, a shower valve.

The state of closeness

A cat walks alone by the road

It looks cared for
but at this moment
it does not care

It is all instinct
overtaken by senses

we humans do not understand

the self-aware connection
we break in our children

We can take care of a cat

We can barely take care
of ourselves.

The summer I was an historical reenactor

Suddenly I'm surrounded
by geese and they're biting me
and they have this way of
dislocating their wings and sort of
punching with them which is
pretty painful and I'm flailing,
yelling at them to go away.

Luckily, Hannah, the staff person
they had imprinted onto, hears
the commotion, comes running over
making some cooing noises and puts
her arm around me, as if to tell them
I am alright, not to mention convincing
me I am alright, and the geese stop
attacking. Slowly they turn but keep
giving me the eye as they totter away,
still not trusting me one bit.

Little Tot Swim Class

They said
Jump
The water
was deep
I knew
I couldn't
They said
Do it
I wasn't
ready
I trusted
them
Jumped
Went
under
Choked
Was rescued
Vomited
Never
returned
Learned
Adults
cannot
be trusted
though
they keep
you alive.
Usually.

First time

She's standing there after doing six pull-ups
with a 25lb weight dangling from her waist.

I'm visiting my son and his fiancée,
who weighs 115 pounds. We are in their garage.

I never saw their workout routine before.
Looking at the bar, I wonder, Can I do one

pullup? I think I can, but am too self-conscious
to even suggest trying. She says

she wants to try 45 pounds, for the first time,
and my son says, *That's pretty heavy, you know,*

and I don't know what to think
as she wraps the belt around her waist,

slips the chain through the center hole
of the big black plate, clips the end link

back to her belt. She stretches to the bar,
hands facing her. I can sense the weight

to overcome, as she takes a tiny hop,
lifts her feet, her legs, her hips,

her torso, her shoulders, her face, her chin
above the bar for a few satisfying seconds,

the weight hanging like a minor annoyance,
still in control, she eases back down.

Baltimore Marathon, mile eighteen

Now slower than mile eight,
or mile twelve,
I am out of the park
passing tall row-homes,
the sky metallic blue,
spectators lining the street
waving posters, shouting,
little kids holding
their adults' hands
as if they knew
this is the hardest part.

Legs moving
will keep moving on their own
until volition
intervenes
or they fail.

A man is giving away
peanut butter sandwiches.
I take one.
The bread
tastes like sawdust.
I toss it stealthily
into a trash barrel.

This stretch
far from the start,
still too far
from the end.

Autobiography

What you see
as my strength
is actually
my hiding
my weakness.

Harlan

Harlan cannot speak
nor walk
nor feed himself.
He was born this way.

Harlan is a great listener.
He watches you
while you speak.
No one knows what he knows.

You can tell him everything
even the things you try
to make go away.
Your secrets are safe.

At least
you have formed the words.
At least
You have told someone.

Steal this poem

Lift the spaces between
the letters and unroll them
backward across the electronic
news ticker of your cerebrum.

By then I will be far away
and not the least maligned,
in fact honored that a shadow
I breathed life into made
its own shadow, with your help.

The way one day spills
into the rest, or the survival
of the fittest, our scavenging
is biblical, exponential,
and without you, at least,
I would disappear.

Volmer

novel by Lise Nørgaard (1917-2023)

A child
    one step ahead of the adults
A sense of the dramatic
A mask
A knot
A turn of a key
    in a lock

What looks like mischief
is a boy's impulse
to reveal
the triumph
of play.

Bumper Riding

Little Mikey walks up Alberta Avenue
after a morning snowstorm
road still half-covered with slush
thinking about his friends talking
about how they grab the rear bumper of a car
slide down the street and then
just let go whenever they want.
And the cars on Alberta are not driving
all that fast, he thinks, and he wonders
how his friends grab onto those cars
and a car comes toward him
in the lane on the other side
of the street and he thinks
if he's quick enough and
he is pretty quick
he can run across and grab
onto the back bumper of that car
and get a cold slide of a ride
whooping down the street, so
without another thought he takes
a quick step into the street
just as a car is coming by
in the near lane, and he doesn't
so much see it as feel it
as he rams right into the side
of that moving vehicle
which propels him backward
like a rag doll
into a big soft pile of snow

by the curb. The car stops.
A door opens and Little Mikey
pops up from the snow bank
and waves to the driver as if
to say, No cause for alarm.
His friends must have
done it differently.

The Last Time

I'm in the house at the shore
watching a baseball game on
the old TV with its enormous
console, the built-in record
player on top and cabinets
for records on both sides,
when my sister enters, angry,
ready to hit or abuse in some
way, as usual, and I am twelve,
now as tall as her, and I just
started lifting weights in the
basement, and I stand up on
the coarse, pale green rug in
my bare feet and push her
away, making a fist with my
right hand, with a cry in
my voice, with my screwed
up face, screaming, "You are
not going to hit me anymore!"
And she just says "Jeez, you
don't have to get so upset,"
as she turns back around
and leaves the room.

Thanksgiving

I was in charge of the gravy.
My son, a better cook,
was roasting garlic cloves
in olive oil
for mashed potatoes.

He saw my gravy,
which was thin, a bit weak,
though I'd followed a recipe
touting "best ever,"
and five-star reviews.

I was reluctant
to modify the gravy,
it would be good
enough, serve a purpose.

My son made the bold move
of removing the lid
and dumping more salt
in the gravy, my gravy,
than I would normally use
in a week.

I held my tongue.
What did I know
about fine cooking?
Now whose gravy was it?

Dinner advanced,
the gravy simmered,
boiled down half an inch
by the time we ate.

A lovely brown,
small bits of
mushroom and onion.
Creamy. Tasty.
Hm.

Perspective function

I thought about it many times
then one day I just did it,
reached out and started playing
with Marla's long layered blonde hair.

It was right in front of me
and Mr De Salis was right
in front of her,
so he couldn't see.

It was in Advanced Calculus
so the class was small
and most everyone could see
what I was doing, playing
with Marla's hair, De Salis
going on about conic sections
and functions approaching infinity.

The other students never spoke
about calculus or Marla's hair,
nor did Marla. I was the only student
who would raise a hand
and ask about the confusing parts
of last night's assignment, and
run my fingers through Marla's hair.

All year it went on like this.
The day before graduation

I ran into Marla in the hall.
We exchanged yearbooks. I asked her
about calculus class. She said she liked it
but it was hard to stay awake.

2

Entering the holy precincts

Anyone can create
the future.

Creating the present
is an entirely
different matter.

My inner universe

A small room
with a bed, a tall chest.

Here it is quiet,
easy to miss sunrise

and sunset, easy
to sleep.

When tired
of sleeping

I watch while
the earth turns.

In a moment of pique
I open a drawer

take out a memory –
white clothing, sunshine

a horse-drawn wagon.
Already I'm exhausted.

I look up.
The drawers reach

floor to ceiling.
I slam it shut.

Earrings

I knew right away they were perfect,
saw them at the outdoor market
a few months after we met.

Dangling earrings in gold, black, and green.
You would look great in these
so I bought them.

Buying jewelry for a woman, not
my wife, not a relative, I stowed them away
for the right moment.

That moment never came. They always felt
too extravagant, which should
have tipped me off.

I learned you don't even wear earrings.
I learned that I had betrayed us all.
Now you and I don't talk anymore.

And I don't know anyone else
who could wear these earrings
the way you could have.

Wisdom

I can’t forgive you.
Not without forgiving myself.

This is what it takes.
To grow through mistakes.

Or maybe not mistakes.
Just life.

Good Dog

There is no shame
in being a dog,
having priorities
signified by a tail,
being precocious
without conscience,
having patience
without regret,
having no filter,
just knowing
what you know,
real reactions
as if every moment
were made for
laughing, crying, napping –
actions we cannot predict
nor prevent,
that's the way
of being
that invites
never growing out of
the way you are.
That's the beauty of it.
No shame
in having four legs
and a tail.

Beekeeper

Formic acid was not legal for use
by a hobby beekeeper like myself.
Thankfully an environmental lab
was generous enough to sell me
a big brown bottle of the stuff.

If you've ever been bitten by ants –
formicidae – you'll know why I wore
heavy nitrile gloves when diluting
formic acid in my beaker and then
saturating my DIY homasote panels.

The bees did not like it
when I inserted the soaked panels.
They buzzed loudly as if their antennae
were burning, but the acid knocked off
mites that suck the bees' body fluids.

The tiny parasites infiltrate the hexagon
cells and weaken the brood, give them
crumpled wings. The mites fell down
through the hive bottom screen to stick
in the vaseline I smeared on the graph

from the extension service so I could
count how many mites, how effective
the treatment, the chances of the hive
surviving the winter. When I moved
to Massachusetts I sold my four hives,

lacking sun in my new yard, not wanting
to deal with bears. I watched the man
strap my hives to a cart as if they were
just animals, as if he had missed
the mystery of their Ural Mountain

heritage, their precarious life cycle,
their potent cooperation when the weather
is right and the locust trees in bloom.
I saw he might never love them,
not the way I did.

Time

The most enormous thing
which does not exist.

Encompasses everything
everyone everywhere

yet is no more than this
ephemeral moment

continually disappearing
while standing still:

Another now, another now.
All the time we have.

Endurance

Between kisses I forget,
so don't stop.

At least,
not until lunch.

Holding pattern

The past is enticing
The future inviting

I can live them
again and again.

Balloon

Get a pin.
I need a way out.
Burst, seep, or ooze.
You have my permis-
sion. So it will sting.
It does anyway. It's
better than keep-
ing contained.
I need to
break.
It
w
o
n
't
t
a
k
e
m
u
c
h

Don't betray yourself

Your great lover was not
who you thought they were.

Love and betrayal appear
together as identical twins.

So buy a soft pretzel
or put on some Bonnie Raitt.

Folly

Basing my worth
on your reaction
is like filling a sieve
with powdered sugar.

I start out so carefully
and the sweetness builds,
but at the least disturbance
I am back where I started –

empty,
and with a mess
to clean up.

Bon Appetit

We cook for each other
to offset the despair.

Yesterday you made
sweet potato peanut soup

sauteed swiss chard
with white beans.

I ate, each swallow
an admission.

As a response I made crepes
with shiitake, spinach and batata,

lettuce and parsley sauce
on the side.

We had no room
for dessert.

Despite Yesterday

Despite yesterday
we see no alternative

to coming back for more.
We don't hurt each other

on purpose. But still
there are plenty of grounds

for giving up. We are that
sensitive, yet overridden

by stubbornness and
niceness. We would never

do that to us. Not if
we haven't yet.

Maybe I shouldn't be writing this down

It is the seventh day
of the seventh month
and last night
you were here for dinner
because your husband was away
and my wife was away –
an unlikely coincidence.

The potato soup was too hot
so we spoke about touch.
I felt like a little boy
craving denied affection
and I wanted to grow up,
release seeking approval
from you, you now a teenager
with several unwanted
admirers at once, badgering
your body into a blockade.

This is our kind of friendship,
bringing all of our selves, the
wanted and the unwanted,
sharing salad dressing recipes,
being at the table, satisfying
and sharpening our hunger.

Pride

I hate how
you always need
full disclosure

Especially about things
that make me
look bad

For example
a bit of pollution
I let slip

A letter from
an old girlfriend
I might not even answer

A customer
who complained
about my thoughtlessness

Though there is
no proof
of actual harm

You want nothing
unmentionable to pass unspoken
to the swamp of memory

And yet
when I swallow my pride
reveal the blemish

Instead of
scorning me
you take me in.

Invitation

We're having a party.
The guest list is
the part of you
that needs something from me
and the part of me
that needs something from you.

They have been best buddies
all these years
coming between us
for better and for worse,
working harder on
our relationship
than ourselves,
until now when
we're ready to celebrate
all they've done.

There will be dancing
around various topics,
sentimental music,
decorations,
finger foods, and
mixed drinks, but
the climax of the evening
will be
when we give them
a set of matching suitcases
for their trip
to a distant island
all expenses paid
one-way.

Late in the afternoon

Things don't turn out
the way you think.

All the prognostications and
fantasies end up in a slag pile
while reality thunders on
to the suppressed surprise
of almost everyone.

We get a few treats
to keep us at least
partly attentive
because we are needed
as guilty bystanders.

That old saying about
being afraid of our power
more than our weakness
is probably true.

Just imagine
if we could change
the future.

Gardener

The way lettuce seedlings cling to the earth
with their tiny rosettes as if there were nothing
but success, potential, days of sun and rain
ahead, a world tilting on its axis just the right
distance from the sun, gently coaxing growth
from the center, up and down, anchored and
blooming, acquainting with nerves, sinews,
breezes and dust. This is what I am nursing.
This is what I make of soil and intention.

3

The Rooster Hour

St. Thomas, US Virgin Islands

It is before dawn
when the cocks begin
crowing, each a response
or echo of the last,
each more hoarse than
the other across multiple
urban and ocean horizons
around the hook of beach
into Charlotte Amalie.
Cacophony continues
well into daylight, inter-
mittently drowned out
by tractor-trailers,
speeding motorcycles,
and thumping ska,
each rooster proclaiming
to the thousands of feral
hens and chicks that this,
this is still their city.

Jossie Gut Sugar Mill

Hans Henrik Berg's Plantation 1820-1862
St. John, US Virgin Islands

The lintels rotted away.
The whips rotted away.

Roots everywhere creep in
from the black portals.

Even with the roof gone
walls still stand.

The sweetness was
exorbitant. And cheap.

A window in 17 Webersgade

Copenhagen, Denmark
Michael Strunge (1958-1986) Danish poet

And that window is where the poet leapt
to his death, said my nephew as we ate pastry
in his kitchen alcove.

Or it might have been the apartment
just above this one. No one here
really knows.

Strunge's fall was nearly forty years ago, and things
are the way they are, which can be mathematically
proven, or nearly.

There is a plaque on the outside wall
commemorating the event with his last words,
"Now I can fly."

I'm not sure I could live there.
The location is excellent, but the view is
nothing special.

All Together Now

There is more
than one place

bombs are striking
without remorse.

The large Earth
keeps us from hearing.

Shrapnel connects
across time.

Once we tried defending ourselves.
Now they try.

Once we died under orders.
Now they die.

There are many hearts
contending for peace.

Pray for mercy.

Café Atlas

We sat with Africa between us,
large and foreboding,
as if it were our responsibility,
that we had done something wrong,
or nothing,
unable to say even
one place name correctly.

When we clinked our glasses
yours fell and broke
on Zanzibar, where your cousin
had his hand chopped off
with a machete.

When we paid I had to
make a snap decision
between credit cards,
didn't know the local
tradition for tipping,
still don't know if
I should have given more.

Far from the fighting

While bombs are being dropped
I am filling my firewood cart
as usual, getting the mail.

Ordinary bombs are falling
while children wait below ground
and I plan my library lecture.

People are hungry for distraction,
for learning how others lead extra-
ordinary lives, disrupting the commonplace.

The newspaper is again in its slot,
while some are praying
for the mundane.

Bystander

Aggression subdues
only half the problem.

Impossible to attack.
Impossible to resist.

The spring of poison
spills and enlivens
like hydra's blood.

Rubble and tanks
are just dead things.

It's the life
that gets you.

Enlistment

I cannot fight
at least I don't think so

I imagine myself
cannon fodder

Mindfully taking
up space

As yet
peaceful and free

A random target
for a munition

So it doesn't destroy
someone else.

Hunger and Thirst

Some fear hunger.
Some fear thirst.

Many wonder
which is worst.

Hunger hurts longer
but thirst kills first.

The legacy of subtle brutality

Don't get used
to feeling loved.

What you don't feel
can't hurt you.

Propaganda

We are bombing
to protect you
from the murderous forces
in your midst
whom you unwittingly
have tolerated. Although
you have been deceived
we know better. We will save
those of you who survive
for a glorious and elevated
civilization based on
the most enduring
declarations.

The Act

We must move on, move on.
What is done is done.
We must bury it with
The future.

What is done is done.
Don't speak or attend to it.
The future
Will set us free.

Don't speak or attend to it.
It will recede like a ship.
And set us free
With distance and forgetting.

It will recede like a ship.
We must move on, move on.
With distance and forgetting
We must bury it.

What we left behind

Dầu Tiếng district, Republic of Vietnam

Family orchard
rubber trees

Teenage son
out weeding

Unearthed
a grenade.

Fabrication

The government was bankrupt
and the neighborhood impoverished.
Someone in the ministry decided
and the military donated a tank,
actually flat-bedded one to the area
and just abandoned it there. It had
been worth millions. The children
played on it first, hid and climbed,
found places to nestle. Artists
anointed it with paint, graffiti
and selectively removed rivets
and panels, which became futons,
lamps, chairs, and sculptures,
mute comments on the industrial.
Time passed, and in desperation
the hungry scavenged fasteners,
rods, sprockets and bushings,
which after thorough rinsing
and baking proved a new source
of nutrition – trace minerals
in particular – which graced many
tables while the tank resembled
more and more a skeleton.

Dancing on the dead

In the absence of nothing
we are leading, being led,

as music is our witness,
our savior and our bread,

with bones a-jangling,
careless, dancing on the dead.

In lieu of prayers
or egos being fed,

we lift up our knees
and prance upon the dead.

Some of them are sad
like a poem never read,

for us to build our floor upon
and dance upon the dead.

There's little better
to revive a troubled head,

than to come together
and dance upon the dead.

Grace period

God is back
after a much-needed
vacation, working
with renewed vigor.

God is starting out
with a positive attitude,
not minding the hours,
enjoying others' praises.

God is going to get
everything working
as well as possible
as soon as possible.

After the war

for *The Halo Trust,* landmine removal

Families wish to return
to their homes.

Soldiers wish to return
to their beds.

Corpses wish to return
to their soil.

There is no going back –
too many mines.

Yesterday
can feel you coming.

Don't get
too close.

Last Rites

I strip off the day's
coarse clothing,
slip under the sheet.

Forgive
what there is to forgive
and go to sleep.

Fragment

I hear the wind blowing
on a pipe
somewhere nearby
creating a coo
like a mourning dove,
as if to remind me
there is something to lament,
there is always
something to lament.

4

Origami Swan

There is no real reason
for anything, except what
came before and maybe
what comes after.

Everything folds
in and out on itself
in directions which may
lead to some surprising
result, which might
be worth saving.

Joyride

If you travel to a place
with an unobstructed view
to the west
at sundown,
stand sideways,
arms stretched out
to the sides
legs spread.

Look down your arm
at the setting sun.
You might be able
to sense the earth
rotating up and away
from the sun
beneath your legs,
carrying you
into the night,
into space,
as fast
as you will ever go.

Another kind of love

Under guise of night –
peace
like a sabbath.

No striving
for sex
or secrets.

Even the incomplete
and the broken
rest.

Slow and cool
darkness displaces
the shadows.

Gravity, Osmosis, and Capillary Action

i.

unless oak galls fall
to the ground
there would be no more
which you might think
does not concern you
until you peel open
the thin globe of skin
see the wee radii
holding the seed of life
then realize maybe
without that you might
never have crawled
and definitely would
not have walked.

ii.

lightning does not happen
all at once, the difference
in charge has to metastasize
its unique path though time
and space before they open
like a door and change
becomes possible.

iii.

the heart dancing in its cage
has its own little gravity, its
own little lightning, as it pushes
its blood out from its fleshy
torso under strict orders until
the extremities take over,
vessels so tiny they have their
own laws where form dictates
content and vice versa.

Tree Bark

Shaggy, grooved, mottled,
scaly, ringed, thorny
or smooth, it is what it is.

Anyone can judge it
ugly, beautiful,
but the fact remains.

In certain light
even wild brokenness
plays equal to elegance.

Time is distancing itself from history

Time is trying to get away from itself,
away from us. It keeps making new days,
new nights filled with voids
which we infallibly occupy
so they can never be reused
or recalled favorably
without sentimentality. It is just
as much time's fault as our own –
it speeds ahead as if death
were on its back, not even a second
to really think, consider consequences,
get underneath where time has been,
before it is buried under new constructions,
like the strata of civilization.
In the time this poem takes,
time is already pulling
you and me in its wake.
The poem nearly forgotten,
and off we go.

Something

When you are without
When those who were supposed to
When you are nonetheless

Then you look for
Then you repress
Then you replace the void with

Sometimes

Sometimes I sink into the mattress
and its molecules get too involved
with mine.

A physicist or a pointillist could prove
that we are actually mixing
on a physical or super-physical plane.

And I have no control over it
except in my mind, which is not
particularly good at objective reality.

I always do get up again, eventually,
but with a feeling of loss or
being diminished.

Then I return to trying
to convince myself
that I am enough.

So I ask you, all this for what?

Words are our downfall.
Even the word downfall
will get you only so far.
Far is a concept within
a system within a culture
and you are trapped there
against your will, as long
as you are subjugated
by words, and who isn't?

However I point to what
is beyond, you can only
see my finger, which is
all I have to point with.
Each of these words
a finger, none of them
a word for what I mean,
no words that liberate us
from the words themselves.

Worth repeating

You do not have to
be original.

Though this point
has been made

since the beginning
of time, patience,

forbearance, say
it again because

not everyone
was paying attention.

Reflection

While you think you are leaving your mark,
you are shaped and fashioned
by the object of your devotion.

Your body conforms
to the movements and postures,
absorbs the stresses and scars,

No less than your mind
does the same with
calculations and processes.

If you wake up wondering who you are,
consider how you have become
the object of your attention.

We are the aliens

With our ten fingers
and ten toes
illogical hair
and central nose.

Populate a planet
in a sector of space
no near neighbors
and not much grace.

The beauty is so infuriating

The beauty keeps rearranging itself
or is it me, rearranging my perception
so I don't go dumb and crazy
staring at the beauty and becoming
generally worthless.

I imagine the beauty starts looking
down on me, criticizing me and
blaming me for getting in its way.
But it's not my fault that nothing
makes sense is a kind of truth.

Beauty doesn't reinvent itself,
it's me who has to do that
more or less every morning,
or else I will just drink my coffee,
go to work and completely
miss the show.

The beauty is a problem
I will not solve in this lifetime.
The beauty is too close,
too omnipresent and too quiet.
It is so small, inside my cells
and totally unperturbed,
ready to triumph
given half a chance.

The Rouge Ford F-150 Factory

Dearborn, Michigan

Aroma of oil, drone of machinery
clacking, shifting, clanging, thudding,
pounding, whining, slowly moving belts,
metal box after metal box, chains, carts,
pallets, each carrying truck parts in various
stages of assembly. People of all sizes and
varieties move from supply case to
assembly line, and again, and again,
holding cords, belts, retainers, rings,
reservoirs, panels, locks, rivets,
bumpers, drills, wrenches, grease-
guns swinging from air hoses,
bolts, screws, glass panes, spacers –
the line inches, grease injected,
bracket attached, nut tightened.
Twelve hundred trucks will roll out
to daylight today from this constant
cacophony, one every fifty-three seconds,
parts moving, hands moving, doors,
cabs, until noon, when the droning,
pounding, and squeaking subsides,
one by one each worker sits down
on an unfinished cab, spreads
out their lunch, and opens their drink.

Vans

Whenever I see a red van
I think of Lenny
the job site manager
I worked with 35 years ago.
Though his van must be
long gone, maybe
Lenny too, to my mind
it might be his. Same thing
with plain white work vans
that make me think of Tim
the electrician I worked with.
Though I know he bought
a bigger truck (also white)
my mind still remembers
his old one. Any brown van
makes me think of Pat
who delivered materials
until he didn't, but my mind
doesn't grasp how time
changes things. And now
silver vans, like yours,
my old friend, seem to be
everywhere, and I always look
for the small dent
on the left rear bumper.

Joy

You practice
something you love
you spend time
with someone you love
you visit
someplace you love
and it's never the same:
sometimes
a let-down
sometimes
same as before
sometimes
rarely sometimes
the experience takes off
in its own direction
and you're swept up
as on a wave
or by a great wind
with a surprised
irrepressible smile
because it is happening
right this moment
and here you are
part of it
riding it
for as long
as it lasts.

My Jazz Band

Grovehill Mansion, historic 1880 residence, Leeds, MA

We set up in the far end of the entry
bass and drums between doors to condos
5 and 6, piano by the stairwell, myself
in front of an antediluvian radiator
large as a water fountain frozen into steel.
Parquet floor in three tones, as exquisite
as if recently installed, heavy wooden
handrail winds above, sculpted infill panels
roll like ocean waves across the balcony.
The audience in chairs along each wall
as if waiting for appointments
with The Duke or The Count.

We launch into June Night, inappropriate
for this January, 81st birthday house party.
The Matron of Honor, who had her hip
replaced seventeen days before, rises,
shuffles a swing dance with her son,
arranger of our concert. Between tunes
she sits back down, says, "That's the most
I've moved since the operation. This
is better than medicine."

As the music swathes the woodwork, swirls
upward to the tower, I flash back to myself
at twenty-one, with a borrowed horn, working

out notes to America the Beautiful, wondering
if I could ever front my own band, embody
the joy I feel when hearing a clarinet swinging
a jazz tune. Thirty-five years later. This.

Things Ain't What They Used To Be

Now's the Time Jazz Ensemble at Luthier's Co-op

At the first notes someone yells,
Oh yeah, that's right
and the room is subtly bobbing
like a kayak on waves
of sound, swing, a cry
rising deep in the soul
of any or all of us,
performers and audience,
for liberation, hunger for
release from responsibility,
from sorrow and soullessness,
tones resonating in our bodies,
a pulse the heart recognizes,
a forgetting and a remembering,
what music does,
Oh yeah, that's right.

That Day Arrived

for Knud Sørensen (1928-2022) Danish author

We do not come from nowhere.
There was someone here before us
who planted seeds
put down roots
looked at the sky
and tried to predict the future.
It is so easy to forget
or assume
that everything starts now.

We are all that came before,
however shameful and joyful,
which we may never live up to.
The story is indelible,
closer than our fingerprints
we are constantly leaving
on everything,
barely a thought to the future,
so caught up in now,
until redeemed by a story.

Knud was a storyteller.
He knew
when a narrative bears weight.
Knud did not write for himself.
He wrote for the story.

He wrote for the timelessness
in the story
so that we would remember
we are more than just this.

WORKS BY MICHAEL FAVALA GOLDMAN

POETRY:

Who has time for this?
Small Sovereign
Slow Phoenix
If you were here you would feel at home
This May Sound Familiar
Someday all of this will be yours
What Minimal Joy
We are more than just this

TRANSLATIONS:

Poetry:

Farming Dreams – Selected Poems of Knud Sørensen
Average Neuroses – Selected Poems of Marianne Koluda Hansen
Inheritance – Selected Poems of Cecil Bødker
Something to Live Up To – Selected Poems of Benny Andersen
Certain Days – Selected Poems of Benny Andersen vol. 2
Selected Poems – Erik Knudsen
New and Selected Poems – Knud Sørensen

Prose:

Fragments of a Mirror – Selected Essays of Knud Sønderby
Stories about Tacit – Cecil Bødker
The Water Farm – Cecil Bødker
Malvina – Cecil Bødker
The Way It Seems – Selected Short Stories of Knud Sørensen
Liberated – Selected Essays of Suzanne Brøgger

The Starveling – Cecil Bødker
Dependency – Tove Ditlevsen
The Trouble with Happiness – Selected Short Stories of Tove Ditlevsen
Stone Upon Stone – Hanne Foighel

CHILDREN'S BOOKS:

Out of the Blue – Rebecca Bach-Lauritsen and Anna Margrethe Kjærgaard

www.ingramcontent.com/pod-product-compliance
Lightning Source LLC
LaVergne TN
LVHW040945150826
845672LV00002B/549

* 9 7 8 8 1 1 9 6 5 4 2 3 9 *